Everything is Fine.

Tylah Virtue

BookLeaf Publishing

Presentation by *BookLeaf Publishing*

Web: www.bookleafpub.com

E-mail: info@bookleafpub.com

ISBN: 9789357616393

First edition 2022

ACKNOWLEDGEMENT

Thank you to anyone who has inspired my thinking and supported my writing.

PREFACE

Out of the ash
I rise with my red hair
And I eat men like air.

- Sylvia Plath

But What's Wrong?

You have nothing
to be sad about
and every reason
to smile
in the streets
and to strangers
you'll never meet,
because we're
all on the
same side.
Our world
is as it
should be,
with everyone
in their rightful
place, and
needed change
underway.
So let's leave
what already
works, staying
the same.
I mean,
what's there
to fix

if nothing
is really
broken?
Don't keep
frowning
when you
can turn it
upside down,
because Love,
everything
in this
world
of ours
is fine.

An Ode

To the abject female body
mutilated and modified
for ample viewing pleasure
with no more left to hide.

To the crowned resident hottie
stylised and sexualised
all for patriarchal leisure
tightly gripping for the ride.

To the blood-soaked oddity
opened wide and objectified
forever unable to measure
the shame clotted divide.

To the hysteria induced lobotomy
paralysed and patronised
a newfound malleable treasure
another victim of misogynistic pride.

Raw

Thinly sliced lips
encircling tongue
cheeks and hearts
tenderised by thumb.

Caressing crevices
sculpting shapes
surfaces splayed
becoming undone.

Trepidation

5

Darling mistress
Thin polish caress
Slick sinned south
Metallic traced mouth
Unassertive unrest

Attested fixation
Vibration insane
Spitfire blade
Hellbent spade
Obliterate with consent

Colourblind gaze
Crimson tide rain
Barbarous angel
Ferocious strangle
Ethical lies ablaze

Automatic fury
Static slain jury
Heroic exploits
Masculine fascination
Routine annihilation

Uncomfortably Dumb

Parabolic garbling of ridicule and rhetoric
by black and white suited soldiers seeking to
pacify and lie through another ballot billed
disguise.

Praise and worship like your pain isn't worth it
and the fight isn't hurting. Instead let yourself be
fooled with grand opium of the mass hypnotise.

Power corrupts absolutely and abuse lingers
resolutely; products of a misuse or miscarriage
passing transgressions on an imperfect marriage.

Pretend this Monday is like last Tuesday, and
ignore
what you think may have happened early
Sunday.
Remember, be passive because the payoff is
massive.

Protect and room service the penchant perverts
padlocked and bleak, being left to neglect
whether they deserved the concealed critique.

Picture-perfect peek into the pleasing and petite
promising, young prey of the week, which will
succumb
to a collective defeat and the inability to ever
speak.

One Evening

Grey skin melts into the waves
Her pale form splayed across the shore
Holes scatter the sand like graves
Exposed to predators, lone and raw
Rendered beaten and poor, she lay
Mites exploring her wired hair
Eyes wide, lips parted to say
Drown me, for I no longer care
Aroused with angst in bitter unrest
Let me plunge over the edge, into the sea
Let me sink the misery numbing my chest
Let me return to you, upheld and free
Instead, her body washed back to life
Unable to escape, sweet widowed wife

A Ballad

Amongst the dry December heat
A deserted rage consumed the air
In our abolitionist age of defeat
We question why this woman would care
To wage a war destined for despair
A salvation motivated for submission
For attaining autonomy mere and rare
Amongst her scorched and seared omission

But don't worry, for there won't be strife
When there was no life alive to begin
The precious, precision of the knife
Against that so called reproductive sin
Piercing and prodding the paper-thin skin
To unearth an unholy underpin birth
And proclaim a solitary seasonal win
For her sacrificial statured self-worth

Burnt

1

Destroying the source
Of our survival
Devastating the future
For restricted revival

Decaying beauty
Of the world we share
Demolishing life
Like we no longer care

Demoralising truths
That shape our fate
Denying the changes
But it is too late

Sinning in the Name Of

She wore snakeskin boots
That night last May
Garnering looks for
Such a brazen display

Two gin and tonics
I offered to pay
We talked with
Nothing left to say

She swallowed my lines
And ideas of foreplay
Accepting she's mine
Assuring her to stay

We exited at half past
Cigarettes in the ashtray
Our bodies moving fast
Steering tonight the right way

Don't question or murmur
Insecure feelings to sway
You're only making me firmer
Our actions must not betray

Here she lay of lust
Legs leading me astray
Stay quiet and trust
That this will all be okay

Haiku For Two

feminine mystique
lies dull, dead and oblique to
the sweet glazed critique

that idiotic
idea of happiness plagues
us chaotically

In the Bath

Another body is succumb to the mud drenched
Liquid cluster lacking luster and vanity
To wash away the apprehension of the day
Fear held at bay to escape the gut-wrench
Trials and miles that invade the clear slate
Of sharpen limbs clean cut by a darken date
Making waves within the porcelain cave
Cultivated for the covert rape of the
Sheer stained satin gown wrapping
Each compact curve designed to avert
The gaze of every perv pouring your tub
With false ideations of love wound
Especially and only for you to fall
Bound into bathing and basting
In moments of hating and wasting
Grounding deeper in the ceramic coffin
Soaked and softened for you to drown
Yet another day and your body in this way.

When the Levee Breaks...again

We never thought
it would get that high
was the collective rhetoric
after the water receded
a time of dire need
left blinded by this belief
and the turmoil that
soon proceeded.
Remorse rippled
through the community
pacing and inundating
homes and childhoods
fighting to not drown
in the sodden remnants
of what was once our town.
If only we had done
more to prepare
and prevent
this may not
have happened the
way that it went.
Sentiments of shame
rage and revenge
was the reaction of

communal inaction
and the inability to
comprehend the
love and lives lost
and the memories
that may submerge
from recollections
of a time past to now
remember and preserve.

Uncovered

Stripping bare the life of 22 years
For the protection of your chauvinistic fears
No vote, no choice, no voice, no control
So you can reach your authoritative goal

Stripping bare the clothes we wear
For the power of the Lord's prayer
No hope left to be heard in a protest
So keep your face hidden while you undress

Keep stripping bare the ethics of equality
For the ferocious fever dreams of frivolity
Let's keep the women oppressed to obey
So we can dictate their death and decay

One Morning

Grey bruises blemish her face
Skin torn for a battle never won
Porcelain shards litter their shared space
Coffee and blood blending into one
Spiteful slurs resound the dining room
Devotion and admiration left behind
Disgust and aversion now consume
Like a reviled creature, alone and confined
You made me do this, you made me mad
Fearing our lives like a feverish dream
You triggered this hate I'd never once had
Searing our minds in a sharpened scream
Silence lingers over remnants of our pain
As your lifeless body is all that will remain

Cash Ruins Everything Around Me

A rigid measure
of our materialistic worth
for the value of sum
to control the earth.
Spiraling to succumb
amongst the immoral hum
of cyclical aggression
and capitalist repression
Buy
Consume
Repeat
Resume
to persist the
placation of billions
Like
Subscribe
Rate
and Bribe
so you're followed
mindlessly by millions
your character recession
sculpturing the building
blocks for another tower
to trump and subjugate

lawful unequal power
feeding status fueled
obsession under the
woke façade of progression.
Believe
Consume
Die
Resume
Spiraling to succumb
till we're ethically numb.

A Limerick

It's time for her monthly menstruation
Linings shed and cyclical ovulation
So be ready for seven days of cramping pains
Remember, ultra-absorbent wings to avoid stains
Against blood censored societal condemnation

Strangler Fig

21

Parasitic bonds and
romantic genocide
of those truly fond
love choked and
sucked dried
a pretty face
remains interlaced
in your wound
web designed
to bed and wed the
heart-shaped hoax
of hunting those
we lust for the most

O entangled fly
who to antagonize?
as in hell we hide
cocooned in quiet
under the guise
and sweet lies of
faux intimacy
displayed with
sick pride when
the game revives
such a toxic divide

But like a strangler fig,
you creep and rise
with such grace
to erase and disgrace
your ensnared prey
suffocating
every inch
of their time
and swallowing
every limb
you must climb
hollowing out
yet another life

A Brief Encounter

Passing by, I catch his gaze
staring me down, observing
my appearance inferior to
his own pressed and
dusted dress. Stern regard
commanding attention
demanding recognition
expecting answers to
his isolated reality
his momentous past
indeterminate future
unreconciled unrest.
I'm sorry, but
I don't know.
My eyes attempt to
commemorate and comfort
the trauma
entrenched in his
I wasn't there
but, I'm here
now.

I move on to the next painting.

An Elegy

The red wine drowns our pain.
Clinking our glasses we drink
beside one another
'cheers' to us together.

Not enough becomes
too many,
and the alcohol soon
drives the scene.
Together we laugh
at this foolish addiction
that drives our life
and defines our bond.

I remember the look
in your eyes that day
of a beautiful pain—
we shared.
Together,
we were whole
enjoying intimate consumption
and exploring tired assumptions.
Infecting and inspiring
each other with light,
and a shattered

darkness,
as the glass
smashes to the floor.

Your body decided
enough is enough
when you fell
from your chair
landing stiff.
My happiness spilt
across the hardwood,
staining
that white shirt
I bought for you
last Christmas.

The broken glass
cut me
as I collapsed too.
Nothing but wine
escaped your breath,
red bleed through your
hair and from your mouth.

I lay next to you
my 'drinking buddy',
on the red stained
polished floor

of the bar we liked.
With our fragmented
glasses still in hand,
clinking one last time
we drown ourselves
once more.

Leather

Time eating what remains
Trapped in a beige tiled cage
Laminate seared with tea stain
Her soiled beauty left in pain
Brittle flowers neat in line
Bleeding hope in near decline
Vision clouded, stale taste
Age shrouded enduring days
Brittle fingers clench the edge
To not seek impending death

Wading grief to stay afloat
Pearls sweep aside her throat
Grey strands decorate tears
Dusting out delicate fears
Intricate shapes will interlace
Gleaming stones to gently trace
Skin like leather worn with joy
Caressing what little left to employ
Precious gems once gifted by him
Withered memories torn thin

Smile Like You're 16 And Don't Mean It

Is there happiness
when everything looks down
Am I happy?
Do I hide it with a frown?

You tell me I'm beautiful
I tell you that's a lie
You tell me not to question it
I simply ask you why

I try to show no pain
and develop no feeling
To avoid heartache
and the process of healing

Infatuated by bliss
and the emotions I see
I question my life
and the way things should be...

9 789357 616393